An Introduction to

Japanese Prints

Joe Earle

Assistant Keeper, Far Eastern Department
Victoria & Albert Museum

V & A / Compton / Pitman House

Designed by Humphrey Stone and edited by Anthony Burton

Photography by Ian Thomas

Printed and bound by New Interlitho SpA, Milan, Italy

ISBN 0 273 01454 4

IT IS NOT generally known that although printing is almost certainly a Chinese invention, the earliest surviving examples of printed text (with the exception of a single Korean charm) are Japanese, dating from A.D. 764, when the empress Shōtoku decreed that a million miniature pagodas should be manufactured and dedicated at leading Buddhist temples. Each pagoda was to contain a Buddhist charm on a slip of paper and the craftsmen entrusted with the task of producing these charms evidently decided to save time by printing them. There is still disagreement as to whether the charms were printed from wood or metal, but what is important for the history of the colour print is that movable type was definitely not used. In this as in all subsequent Japanese printing, except for a brief phase from about 1590 to about 1650, the impressions were taken from wood blocks carved (or perhaps, in this unique case, metal plates cast) specially for each page of text, and the experience built up over centuries of carving the intricate Japanese script formed a significant part of the technological inheritance drawn on by the men who made the blocks for the prints of the Edo period (1615–1868), with which we are chiefly concerned here.

For about three hundred years from 764 there is no evidence of printing in Japan but in 985 a complete printed copy of the huge Buddhist canon known as the *tripitaka* was brought from China by a Japanese pilgrim. This impressive publishing feat appears to have rekindled monkish interest in printing and in 1088 the first Japanese printed Buddhist text appeared. About one hundred years later we find woodblocks used for illustration for the first time in a series of decorated fan leaves in which certain repeated details were mass-produced by the use of hand-held stamps and in the same century decorative backgrounds were added to scrolls by similar means.

The popular sects of Buddhism which gained recognition during the twelfth and thirteenth centuries, with their emphasis on repeated invocations of the name of the Buddha, were a stimulus to

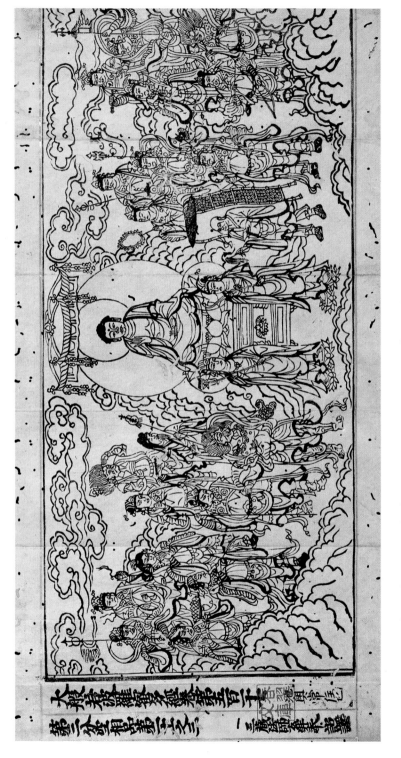

PLATE I Anonymous, after a Chinese original. The pilgrim Hsüan Tsang receiving the *tripiṭaka* canon from the Buddha. Frontispiece to volume 517 of the *Dai Hannya-Haramitta-Kyō*, a Buddhist scripture. Printed from wood blocks, probably at Kōfukuji temple, Nara. Dated 1383. 26.2 × 47 cms (10.3 × 18.5")
F.E.107–1975 Hofer Gift

the development of printed illustration. Scrolls and sheets of paper were stamped with innumerable identical images of the deity to the order of devotees eager to buy them as a quick and convenient method of accumulating merit. These popular printed icons grew considerably more elaborate and some of the later examples exhibit a high degree of skill in block-cutting and printing. At the same time an increasing number of Buddhist texts came to be illustrated with frontispieces, usually inspired by Chinese models (PLATE 1), while in the early fifteenth century printed handscrolls with illustrations in native Japanese style made their first appearance.

The printed works mentioned so far were all of Buddhist origin; until about 1590 the Japanese printing industry was dominated by the temples and monasteries. But from that time on there was a dramatic expansion of publishing activity in the field of secular illustrated fiction which led to the appearance, probably around 1680, of independently printed designs, the first 'Japanese prints' in the sense in which those words are normally used today. These were printed in black but even in the earliest examples we find that colours, especially red lead (*tan*) and yellow were often added by hand, a practice which persisted until about 1715 when another red, of vegetable origin, called *beni*, was introduced. A little later it became fashionable to add lacquer and sprinkled brass dust to create a more luxurious effect and to highlight certain areas of the print (see PLATE 6 for a well preserved example). Then, in the early 1740s, *beni* red and green were for the first time applied to prints by using specially cut extra wooden blocks.

In books, as opposed to independent prints, colour printing had been used as early as 1631 in the diagrams for a mathematical treatise and during the eighteenth century an increasing range of colours was printed on the illustrations to books of poems, painting manuals and other publications. But these early efforts were privately printed for select circles of connoisseurs and were inspired by Chinese models; it was not until the mid-1760s that a development occurred which ushered in the age of full-colour printing in a purely Japanese style for a wide public. At the end of 1764 a small group of art-lovers decided to commission full-colour illustrated calendars for the following year, and they employed to design these a little-known artist called Suzuki Harunobu (PLATE 7), who was encouraged by the new techniques available to develop a novel style which was to make him one of the great names in the history of the Japanese print. Soon the calendars were republished as straightforward prints (without dates) and the age of popular colour printing had begun.

The traditional print was a result of the collaboration of three distinct specialists: the designer, the blockcutter and the printer. The lion's share of the credit for the finished article has always gone to the designer, by whose name the prints are known, but the contribution of the other two craftsmen was at least as great. Much of the beauty of Japanese prints lies in qualities which have in recent years become harder to appreciate now that most of us experience them through the barrier of photographic reproduction and it is just these qualities which are due to the blockcutter and the printer: the clarity and depth of the colours, the sharp precision of the details and the look and feel of the *hōsho* paper, made from the inner bark of the mulberry tree, which is soft and yet strong enough to remain stable over as many as ten printings. The efforts of these three craftsmen were coordinated by the publisher. The greatest publishers, for example Tsutaya Jūsaburō (1750–1797) could influence the whole course of the *ukiyoe* movement; Tsutaya 'discovered' or encouraged such artists as Utamaro (PLATE 11) and Sharaku and was a dominant figure during one of the great periods of the art.

The production process began with the designer, who painted a detailed line drawing on specially thin paper in a mixture of soot and glue. Occasionally this job was not done by the artist in person but entrusted to another craftsman, who set down in detail the artist's rough sketch. The completed drawing was then passed to a team of blockmakers, whose task was to interpret the designer's wishes in woodblock form. The drawing was sized to prevent wrinkling and carefully pasted face-down on to a block. The back of the paper was scraped away so that only a very thin layer was left and this remaining layer was then oiled leaving the drawing fully visible to the blockcarver. All the surface of the block was then cut away except the lines of the drawing. The job of cutting round the lines was reserved for the senior member of the carving team, who used a knife with an angled blade. Then a chisel with a rounded head was used to clear waste wood away from the areas adjacent to the cut line, thereby facilitating the more general clearing done with larger chisels. The blocks themselves were of cherrywood, cut with the grain (this yields larger blocks than end-grain cutting), seasoned for several years in clamps and then meticulously planed.

An important feature of the line block left by the first stage of cutting is the pair of marks, one at a corner and one in the middle of a side, which were used to ensure perfect registration when the colour blocks were printed. Once completed the line-block was used to produce a number of impressions (incorporating these marks) on which the designer indicated the colours he wanted for each area of the print. Colour blocks were then cut and the prints were run off.

The Japanese printing method differed considerably from the Western, above all in the fact that the paper was placed on the block (instead of the block on the paper) and rubbed on the back with a circular pad made from bamboo. It is the use of this rubbing technique, combined with the softness of the paper, which gives the colours in Japanese prints their texture and depth; often, in fact, the colours are clearly visible on the reverse. The inks used were *sumi*, the soot and glue mixture used for the original design, and a variety of vegetable and mineral pigments mixed on the block itself before each printing. Special techniques include 'blind-printing' without ink, which embosses the paper, and the wiping of colour blocks before printing so that the colour varies in intensity in the finished print.

There is an almost defiant bravura in the technical virtuosity of some of the later carvers and printers, whose intention is clearly to transcend rather than to be faithful to the woodblock medium (see, for example, PLATE 26). In the present century, however, artists of the *sōsaku hanga* (Creative Print) movement, who carry out every stage of the process themselves, have felt the need to be honest to their materials and let the process show in the finished print. It is with a work by one of these artists that the present selection concludes.

THE BACKGROUND AND DEVELOPMENT OF THE UKIYOE STYLE

The stylistic origins of the Edo period prints are complex and to trace them in full it is necessary to go back several hundred years to the narrative scrolls in which the native pictorial style came to maturity. In these scrolls the emphasis is always on decorative effect, with strong and gorgeous colour and well-defined outlines. The early Muromachi period (fourteenth and fifteenth centuries), in which contact with Chinese civilisation was renewed after a period of isolation, saw the introduction by Zen Buddhist monks of a bold style of monochrome ink-painting, chiefly of Chinese subjects, and for some time the two schools, one native Japanese and the other of Chinese origin, remained strictly separate. In the mid-sixteenth century, as the chaotic military conditions which had prevailed for two hundred years began to improve, the numerous warlords started to commission paintings for the gloomy halls of their newly-built castles. Many of these warlords were of humble origin and were interested neither in exquisite miniaturist depictions of a vanished court life nor in the austere brushwork of the Zen monks and in response to their demands a new and splendid style emerged which combined the graphic boldness of the Chinese brush-manner with the sumptuous colouring of the native tradition. The pairs of sixfold screens and the sliding doors which were adorned in this new way are one of the crowning glories of the Momoyama period (1568–1615) and indeed of all Japanese pictorial art.

To begin with, the subject-matter of these screens was confined to Chinese sages, scenes from classical legend and symbolic birds and flowers, but the painters gradually began to turn their attention to the daily life of the time and to paint such subjects as maple-viewing parties, festivals at famous shrines, views of life in and around the capital, Kyoto, or the strange Portuguese missionaries and Dutch traders who at this time intruded briefly into Japanese history. An important contemporary stimulus to the emergence of a new genre style was provided by the *Nara-e* paintings, a popular offshoot of the narrative scroll tradition, many of which show a lively concern with the affairs of ordinary people. They are another path by which the old styles of painting were applied to new subject-matter and made accessible to a wider audience.

The most important influences, however, on the development of the Japanese print were undoubtedly social and economic. The period 1550–1650 saw a general improvement in material prosperity which stimulated demand for artefacts of all kinds and also provided artists with a whole new world of subject-matter. By 1615 the entire country had been unified by Tokugawa Ieyasu, who moved the capital from Kyoto to Edo (modern Tokyo) and founded a dynasty of military rulers which controlled Japan until the 1860s. The resulting peace was accompanied by the introduction of a money economy and the growth of a number of bustling urban centres where the newly-prosperous merchant and artisan classes, deprived by a rigid hierarchy of the chance to use their wealth to improve their social status, began to develop their own distinctive culture of which the most striking features, from the point of view of print history, were the brothels and the theatres. A general increase in literacy among the urban classes resulted in a surge of publishing activity: Buddhistic novellas, guide books, tales based on the plots of puppet dramas and classical Japanese romances appeared in large numbers. Until about 1660 the illustrations were for the most part in the traditional narrative style, but during the same period a new kind of painting was developing from the combined Chinese/Japanese school of the late sixteenth and early seventeenth centuries. It took as its subject-matter the denizens of the newly-flourishing gay quarters

PLATE 2
Hishikawa Moronobu (*c.* 1618–1694)
Watanabe no Tsuna visited by the demon of Rashōmon
disguised as a nurse. *c.* 1680–1690.
25.1 × 34.6 cms (9.9 × 13.6″)
E.1346–1922   Lee Bequest

9

and in time both the new milieu and the paintings were referred to by a special term, *ukiyo*. This was originally a Buddhist expression meaning 'this sad world', but by about 1660 the character for the *uki* part of the word had been changed to give the meaning 'floating world', with connotations of rapidly changing fads and fashions, optimism and a general lack of thought for the morrow. Add *e*, meaning pictures, and you have *ukiyoe*, 'pictures of the floating world', the term normally used for pictorial art in this style by the Japanese themselves. The first artist (or at any rate the first artist known to us by name) to adopt this floating-world painting and combine it with the classical narrative style to produce an entirely new type of book-illustration was Hishikawa Moronobu (PLATE 2); and around 1680, as mentioned above, these illustrations began to appear in independent form.

Moronobu's talent for composition is clearly evident in the print reproduced here; another feature of his style which is not so well represented is the striking exploitation of the contrast between mass and line, for example between the solid black mass of a girl's hair and the bounding lines and complicated arabesques of her costume. It is Moronobu's use of the limitations imposed by the stark choice of black or white which has gained him the admiration of many collectors, sometimes at the expense of the multicoloured prints of the later period.

The print shows the well-known story of Watanabe no Tsuna, who cut off a demon's arm in a fight. Disguised as Watanabe's old nurse, the demon tricked the hero into producing the arm. It then seized its severed limb and flew off screaming into the air. The subject matter allows rather close adherence to traditional narrative methods: strong diagonals and roofs left off buildings to show indoor action.

It is as well to mention, before discussing the subsequent development of *ukiyoe*, that this book, which deals only with independent prints, gives a very one sided impression. A vital contribution continued to be made by both illustrated books and paintings and many of the artists discussed below were distinguished in both these additional fields. Another type of print which is inadequately treated here is the *shunga*, erotica, although these too constitute a large part of the oeuvre of many of the most famous artists (PLATE 10). The reader should also be reminded that a number of print-designers, of whom the most prominent is perhaps Sharaku (active 1794–5), are not represented in the Victoria and Albert Museum's collections.

For a hundred years and more the subject-matter of the print was dominated by actors and courtesans. After an unsteady start, during which first women actors and then, in 1652, young boys were banned from the stage by the authorities, the popular·*kabuki* theatre developed rapidly, with specially trained adult males taking the female parts. The *kabuki* is very much a theatre of virtuoso actors and it is the style of acting, rather than the stories, which constitutes its single most distinctive feature. The actors could, if they were successful, become extremely rich; their life-styles excited the admiration of the populace and, on occasion, the wrath of the authorities, who attempted to restrain high living by sumptuary edicts and other restrictions. Given the glamorous position which the actors held (comparable with that of film-stars in the Hollywood era), it was natural that they should be an important source of subject-matter for print designers.

For fifty years the actor print was the special domain of the Torii family of designers, prints by two of whom, Kiyonobu and Kiyomitsu, are reproduced here (PLATES 3 and 4). Kiyonobu was born in Osaka, the son of a man who painted signboards for *kabuki* theatres, but in 1687 the family moved to Edo and the influence of Moronobu is evident in many of Kiyonobu's prints. On his father's death in 1702 Kiyonobu became head of the school; in fact, he is usually regarded as the founding father of the actor print. In the present example, which can be dated to around 1725 on the basis of theatrical records (the actors themselves being identified by the signs on their costumes), Kiyonobu has left behind the influence of Moronobu and has established a monumental, iconic style, with more attention given to the fall of draperies and the pose than to individual facial expression. This style was to dominate the actor print for much of the next forty years, as we can see from the print of about 1760 by Kiyomitsu, the third master of the Torii line.

Katsukawa Terushige, an obscure artist who was probably a pupil of Kiyonobu, was the designer of our first print (PLATE 5) depicting a scene in the Yoshiwara, the pleasure quarter of Edo, a world unto itself where class barriers between merchants, *samurai* (who were legally barred but entered regularly under the thinnest of disguises) and actors lost their meaning. Although the best quality girls were extremely expensive, money was by no means everything in the Yoshiwara and the higher class courtesans could spurn with impunity the advances of a rich but boorish client. As well as providing the services which would be expected of them all over the world, the courtesans were often accomplished musicians, versifiers and conversationalists and the best of them might in time be able to save enough money to buy themselves out or even to marry a rich admirer. The print shows a girl and her lover warming themselves at a *kotatsu*, a kind of covered stove. The youth, whose sword lies in the background, holds a pipe in one hand and in the other a note,

PLATE 3
Torii Kiyonobu (1664–1729)
The actors Sodezaki Iseno as a
girl embraced by Ogino Isaburō
as a samurai
Handcoloured and decorated with
brass dust
Publisher's mark and seal
Signed *Torii Kiyonobu hitsu*
c. 1726
31.75 × 15.2 cms (12.5 × 6″)
E.53–1895

PLATE 4
Torii Kiyomitsu (1735–1785)
Portrait of the actor *Sakata
Hangorō* I as *Yamada Saburō*
Inscribed with a poem
Publisher's marks and seal
Signed *Torii Kiyomitsu ga*
c. 1760
31.4 × 14.6 cms (22.25 × 5.75″)
E.289–1952   Shipman Bequest

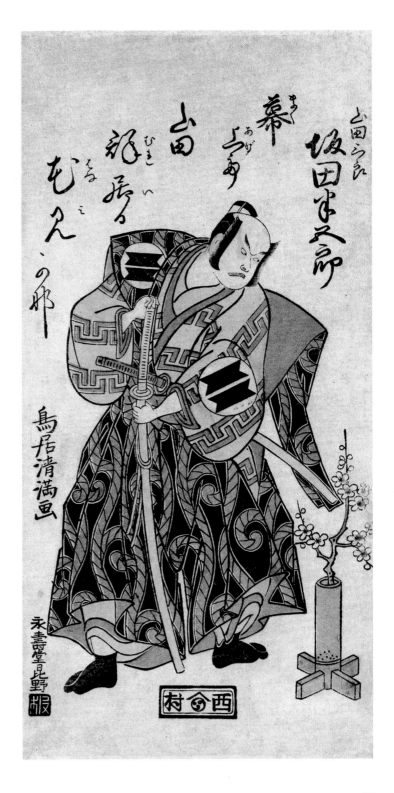

PLATE 5
Katsukawa Terushige (active *c.* 1715–*c.* 1725). Couple warming
themselves by a *kotatsu*. Handcoloured. A poem has been added in
manuscript. Publisher's jar-shaped mark. The painting in the alcove
signed *Katsukawa Teru*. Signed on the screen *Katsukawa Terushige*.
20.3 × 29.2 cms (8 × 11.5")
E.609–1899

presumably a love letter. The contrast between the flowing draperies of the foreground and the angular architecture of the background is a constantly recurring feature in these eighteenth century interior views. One owner of the print must have thought that the lover was about to take his leave, for the Chinese poem, sketched in at some time in a none too well-educated hand, includes the line 'I must return from the green houses . . .'. The brothels were so named from their typical external colouring.

The splendidly preserved print in PLATE 6 is a perfect example of the gentle world of Okumura Toshinobu. A figure on horseback, identified as a *samurai* by the exaggeratedly long hilts of his two swords, is being led astray by a lady of the Yoshiwara. The *samurai* points to his left in mild protest but he is no match for the girl, whose name, *Nowaki* (autumn hurricane), suggests determined passions.

Suzuki Harunobu (PLATE 7) was the artist who ushered in the age of full-colour printing for a wide audience, but that was by no means his only contribution to the Japanese print. He created a new world of delicate feeling, conveyed above all by his refined colour schemes and the sweet expressions of the nymph-like girls who people his prints; these are very often not habituées of the Yoshiwara but simply girls of Edo going about their daily business. PLATE 7 reproduces a sheet from a famous series of his; the expression 'eight views' in the title referred originally to a scenic area of China but its use by the print designers as an excuse for sets of views of everyday life is typical of their playful attitude towards classical tradition. It is interesting to note how different the colours are from those of the original edition (published a year or two earlier, *c.* 1766) and yet how entirely effective: this variation of colour-scheme from state to state is a feature of many famous prints but we shall probably never know to what extent it is due to the wishes of the artist rather than the experimentation of the printer.

Isoda Koryūsai, another artist of this early period of full colour, is represented by two prints in his favourite format, the long and narrow *hashirae*: he exploited the difficulties of the shape with triumphant success. In the charming study of a girl teasing her dog, very skilful use is made of the long handle of the musical instrument to create a strong and yet unobtrusive diagonal which holds together the widely separated elements of the composition (PLATE 8).

Torii Kiyonaga (PLATE 9) was a pupil of Kiyomitsu, but his theatrical prints do not form an important part of his work. Tall, stately beauties were his speciality and he was fond of displaying them in groups out of doors, where a carefully conceived background could be used to add interest to a colourful and statuesque display of courtesans languidly engaged in trivial pursuits. The courtesan print was dominated by his work throughout the 1780s and some elements of his style survived long into the nineteenth century, but Kiyonaga himself appears to have given up print designing in the early 1790s.

Shunga, erotica, were mentioned above as a neglected aspect of the work of many artists (including, incidentally, Kiyonaga, for all the chilly elegance of the women in his more normal work). Mainly because of the often grotesquely exaggerated size of the sexual organs many *shunga* seem ridiculous to our eyes, but Shunchō's print (PLATE 10) is reasonably free of this defect. To the modern viewer, at any rate, this is a decidedly unpornographic and sensitive scene.

Utamaro (PLATE 11) dominated the 1790s as Kiyonaga had the previous decade. He is one of the great print artists of the world and his achievements were many but it is perhaps for the expressiveness of his depiction of female beauty that he is most admired today. Neither Harunobu, for all his pretty charm, nor Kiyonaga, for all his stately grandeur, had inspired their subjects with much in the way of individual character, but Utamaro goes beneath the surface to produce beauties whose distinctive personalities are transmitted to the viewer with the utmost economy and subtlety.

Utamaro's influence was great and many of his contemporaries designed prints which can bear comparison with his own master-pieces. Three are reproduced here, all of them dating from around the middle of Utamaro's great decade. PLATE 12 shows a famous design of Chōbunsai Eishi, who is unique among the great *ukiyoe* artists in that he was the son of a high official of the government – in other words he was of *samurai* rather than plebeian origin. The pro-nounced elongation of the figure (a feature of many of Utamaro's prints of the same date) and the rather haughty expression do not encourage us to warm to Itsutomi's human qualitites – Eishi is less of an observer of human nature than his great contemporary – but the superb decorative quality (enhanced here by a mica-printed back-ground) and splendid composition more than compensate for any lack of psychological insight. This is the golden age of the *ōkubie* (bust portrait), and although Utamaro is its greatest master he had in Hosoda Eishō (PLATE 13) a worthy rival, both in composition and in skill in conveying a sense of volume to the faces, a sense conveyed by line alone, without the help of light and shade. The advanced level of printing technique, still free from the evil effects of overproduc-tion and garish dyes, is well illustrated by the superb depiction of the semi-transparent fan and comb. Eishōsai Chōki (PLATE 14) had a penchant for the half-length portrait (a compromise between the

PLATE 7
Suzuki Harunobu (died 1770)
Returning sails of the towel rack,
from the series *Zashiki Hakkei,*
eight views of the parlour
c. 1768
26.4 × 20.6 cms (10.4 × 8.1″)
E.55–1955

PLATE 8a
Isoda Koryūsai
(active *c.* 1764–1780s)
Girl teasing her dog with a *samisen*
Hashirae (pillar-print)
Signed *Koryūsai ga* with a seal
Masakatsu
c. 1775
69.5 × 12.1 cms (27.4 × 4.75″)
E.3756–1953   Horn Bequest

PLATE 8b
Isoda Koryūsai
A courtesan's lucky dream
Hashirae (pillar-print)
Signed *Koryū ga*
69.5 × 12.1 (27.4 × 4.75″)
E.3757–1953   Horn Bequest

PLATE 9 Torii Kiyonaga (1752–1815)
A walk in the suburbs. Publisher's marks. Signed on each sheet *Kiyonaga ga*
1780s. 38.7 × 76.2 cms (15.25 × 30″). E.392–1895

PLATE 10 Katsukawa Shunchō (active *c.* 1780–*c.* 1795)
Lovers on a balcony, from the series *Kōshoku zue junikō*, the twelve hours
of lovemaking, illustrated. 1790s. 24.8 × 37.4 cms (9.75 × 14.7″) E.225–1968

ōkubie and the statuesque full-length courtesans typified by Eishi's print) and he was especially fond of giving his figures an atmospheric background such as a night sky filled with fireflies, a fall of snow or, as here, a gently rippling sea contrasting sharply with a mica-decorated sky and a strongly coloured sun. The setting of the figure against the background is the key to the marvellous compositional unity of this design, a unity which is underlined by the choice of colour for background and foreground. This is a print of which many varying states exist, with marked differences in background detail and even in the mood suggested by the girl's face. In the copy illustrated the unity of the girl and her setting seems to be enhanced by her expression, which conveys a sense of refined expectation entirely appropriate to the first day of the year.

By 1760, the approximate date of Kiyomitsu's print (PLATE 4), the actor portrait seemed to have entered a stylistic groove from which it might never emerge, but ten years later, in 1770, the transformation of this particular area of *ukiyoe* art was heralded by the publication of *Ehon Butai no Ōgi*, a picture book of fans for the stage, designed by Ippitsusai Bunchō and Katsukawa Shunshō, which consists of three volumes of bust portraits of actors on fan-shaped backgrounds. Unlike most previous actor prints the portraits by these two artists were individually characterised; from then on it would no longer be necessary to identify actors by the crests on their costumes or by inscriptions giving their names. In his actor prints Shunshō stresses too the dramatic qualities inherent in each theatrical situation: in the triptych reproduced here (PLATE 15), it seems clear enough that the two flanking figures are rivals for the affections of the central courtesan and each face expresses the appropriate emotion as well as being recognisable as that of a known individual actor. It is noteworthy that Shunshō did not limit himself to depicting actors on the stage; in his pursuit of the individual character of each star he went behind the scenes for some perceptive studies of actors preparing in their dressing rooms or relaxing at home.

A favourite role of the Ichikawa Danjūrō line of actors was the interlude known as *Shibaraku*, 'wait a moment!'. This interlude, in which a fearless *samurai* rescues a young couple from execution, was invented in 1697 by the first Danjūrō and performed by members of the Ichikawa family on countless occasions from then on. Few actor-print artists could resist the temptation of the design possibilities offered by the striking striped make-up, the great badges of the Ichikawa family and the comically huge sword. Utagawa Toyokuni (PLATE 16) alone is known to have produced several prints of the subject. The print shows Ichikawa Danjūrō VII, perhaps the supreme theatrical giant of the nineteenth century, in his debut

PLATE 11
Kitagawa Utamaro (1754–1806)
Yoso iku no kihan, boats returning from a visit to another place, from the series *Fūzoku ukiyo hakkei*, up-to-date eight views of the floating world
Publisher's mark
Signed *Utamaro hitsu*
Early 1790s
38.1 × 25.1 cms (15 × 9.9")
E.3244–1953   Lee Bequest

22

△ **PLATE 13** Hosoda Eishō (active *c.* 1780–*c.* 1800). **The courtesan** *Yosooi* **of the** *Matsubaya.* Publisher's mark. Signed *Shōeidō Eishō ga.* **1790s**
38.4 × 25.4 cms (15.1 × 10″). E.1414–1898

◁ **PLATE 12** Chōbunsai Eishi (1756–1829). **The courtesan** *Itsutomi* **holding the plectrum for a samisen which lies behind her, from the series** *Seirō geisha sen,* **selected entertainers of the green houses.** Publisher's mark, censor's seal Signed *Eishi zu. c.* 1795. 39.4 × 26 cms (15.5 × 10.2″). E.3762–1953
Horn Bequest

26

as a fully-fledged actor; to honour the occasion a congratulatory poem is inscribed above.

Most of the prints discussed here are by artists who lived in Edo, but it seems only just that the great Osaka tradition of theatrical print design should be represented by one example (PLATE 17) which illustrates well the distinctive style of the great commercial centre of western Japan. The abiding influence of Shunshō can be seen in the individuality and drama of the face – a feature which Hokushū in fact intensified in this striking portrait of another great actor, Nakamura Utaemon III. The use of the fan to concentrate attention on the facial expression is a favourite Osaka device; and mirrors and circular reserves were frequently used in the same way.

The demand for actor prints and pictures of courtesans continued throughout the nineteenth century, but although many splendid designs were produced in response to this demand they are not the most characteristic products of the age and it is not by them that the later period of *ukiyoe* is best known. From about 1820 onwards the most important and most innovative prints are the landscapes, the warrior prints and, to a lesser extent, the bird and flower studies and the still-lifes. When, in the 1850s and 1860s, European contact with Japan was resumed, the first *ukiyoe* prints to reach artists in Paris and London were those which were currently for sale on the streets of Edo and Yokohama so that even today Hokusai, Hiroshige and Kuniyoshi, the great nineteenth century trio, are better known to most westerners than the masters of the eighteenth century, with the possible exception of Utamaro. The two Japanese prints most famous in the West are probably the *Great Wave off Kanagawa* and the *Fuji in Clear Weather* (PLATE 18) both by Hokusai. But as we marvel at the majestic simplicity of the design we would do well to remember that Hokusai had been artistically active for more than forty years when it was published; he had done actor prints in the style of Shunshō and beauties under the influence of Kiyonaga; he had established the *surimono* greeting cards (see below) as an important minor art form and he had produced countless sketches and illustrated books. Many of these aspects of his work are only a little better appreciated today than they were at the end of the nineteenth century.

If Hokusai's landscapes are celebrated above all for the almost abstract grandeur and simplicity of their design, for the skill with which all inessentials are cut away in the interests of total effect, we admire his great contemporary and successor Hiroshige for sensitive depiction of the everchanging moods of nature and sympathetic portrayal of man in his physical environment. Hiroshige is the great master of rain, whether it be the squally showers in his famous

PLATE 14
Eishōsai Chōki
(active *c.* 1786–*c.* 1805)
Sunrise on New Year's Day
Publisher's mark, censor's seal
Signed *Chōki ga*
1790s
38.7 × 24.8 cms (15.25 × 9.75")
E.3774–1953   Horn Bequest

△ PLATE 15
Katsukawa Shunshō (1726–1792). Scene from a play
Left to right: Ichikawa Danjūrō V, Segawa Kikunojō, Ichimura
Uzaemon. Signed on each sheet, *Shunshō ga. c.* 1780.
30.5 × 42.9 cms (12 × 16.9″). E.1282–1896

▷ PLATE 16
Utagawa Toyokuni (1769–1825). The actor *Ichikawa Danjūrō* VII in
a *shibaraku* role. Inscribed with a poem. Publisher's mark, censor's seal
Signed *Toyokuni ga.* 1807. 38.7 × 27.3 cms (15.25 × 10.75″)
E.12646–1886

28

PLATE 17
Shunkōsai Hokushū
(active 1810– 1832)
The actor *Nakamura Utaemon* III
as *Kyōgoku Takumi* in the play
*Hikosan gongen chikai no
sukedachi* which was performed at
the Kadono theatre, Osaka, in
March–April 1825
Publisher's mark and seal
Signed *Shunkōsai Hokushū ga* with
a seal *Hokushū*
1825
36.8 × 25.4 cms (14.5 × 10″)
E.1321–1922   Lee Bequest

print of *Shōno*, with travellers rushing for shelter, or the long
drenching downpour of *Night Rain at Karasaki* from the *Eight Views
of Lake Biwa*. He captured the atmosphere of this latter print again in
a fan print (PLATE 19), *Night Rain at Eitai Bridge*, where the atmosphere of overpowering stillness broken only by the sound of rain
falling is emphasised – a typical Hiroshige touch – by the presence
of bowed figures in straw hats and raincoats poling their vessels.
Hiroshige is best known, perhaps, for his two great landscape and
travel series, *The Fifty-three Stations on the Tōkaidō Road* and the
Sixty-nine Stations on the Kisokaidō Road (the latter set done in collaboration with a lesser artist, Keisai Eisen). To represent these another
weather dominated scene has been chosen (PLATE 20); as in
Hiroshige's studies of rain the skill and patience of the block-cutters
contributes much to the effect, but it is the treatment of the human
figures which lends the print its special atmosphere.

   This brief selection of landscapes concludes with Yashima Gakutei,
a lesser-known artist, whose work shows the influence of Hokusai,
sometimes in direct adaptation of the master's designs, sometimes
merely in the quasi-geometric simplicity of approach. In the 1830s
Gakutei lived in Osaka, whose local scenery inspired him to produce
his best-known series, the views of Mount Tempō. The brilliantly
effective colour scheme and quiet grandeur of PLATE 21 place it
almost on a level with some of Hokusai's greatest designs.

   It was explained above that the commissioning of calendar prints
for private circulation encouraged the development of full-colour
printing in *ukiyoe* style; in fact these calendars have a double impor-
tance, for there also developed from them a tradition of privately
printed greeting cards of all kinds which formed a significant part
of print production during the late eighteenth and early nineteenth
centuries. These special prints, called *surimono* (meaning no more
than 'rubbed [i.e. printed Japanese-style] thing') were published in
small numbers and not sold on the open market. They were com-
missioned by wealthy men and were usually sent on special occasions. For all these reasons a great deal of care and attention was
lavished on their production, with extreme precision in the printing,
great subtlety of colouring and liberal use of such techniques as
blind-printing and decoration with metal dusts. That indefatigable
innovator Hokusai was largely responsible, it seems, for the spread
in popularity of these exquisitely-printed items but we reproduce
here a print by a lesser-known artist, Kubo Shumman (PLATE 22)
who made something of a speciality of them. Typical features include bold use of blind printing and poems, presumably by members
of the charmingly named 'Mist Club' which appears to have com-
missioned the series.

PLATE 18 Katsushika Hokusai (1760–1849). *Gaifū kaisei*, a gentle breeze and clear weather,
from *Fugaku sanjūrokkei*, thirty-six views of Mount Fuji. Signed *Hokusai aratame Iitsu hitsu*
Late 1820s. 24.8 × 36.2 cms (9.75 × 14.25″). E.4813–1916. Alexander Gift

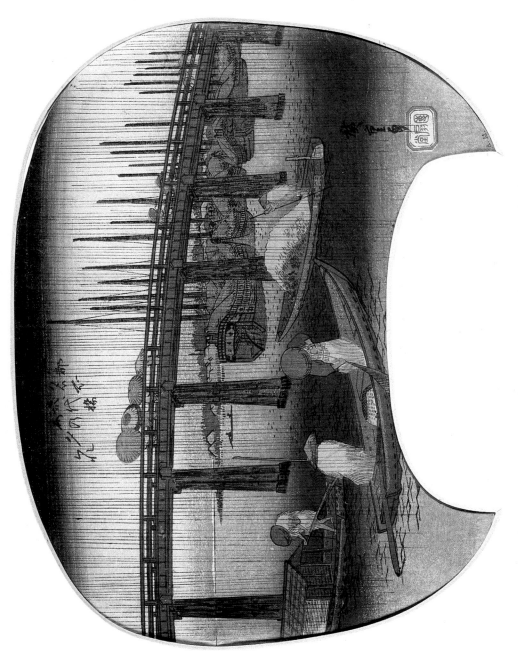

PLATE 19 Andō Hiroshige (1797–1858). Night rain at Eitai bridge from a
series Kōto meisho, views of Edo (Tokyo). Publisher's seal. Signed Hiroshige ga
c. 1840. 22.2 × 29.5 cms (8.75 × 11.6"). E.4938–1919

PLATE 20 Andō Hiroshige (1797–1858) Ōi, number 47 from the series *Kisokaidō rokujūkyū tsugi no uchi*, from the 69 stations on the Kisokaidō road. Publisher's and censor's seals. Signed *Hiroshige ga* with a seal *Ichiryūsai. c.* 1840. 26 × 36.8 cms (10.25 × 14.5″). E.3802–1886

PLATE 21 Yashima Gakutei (*c.* 1786–1868). *Tempōzan mansen nyūshin no zu*, fleet of ships entering Tempōzan harbour from the series *Tempōzan shōkei ichiran*, views of Mt Tempō. Signed *Gogaku* with a mark. 1830s. 25.2 × 36.8 cms (10 × 14.5″). E.745–1910

△ PLATE 22   Kubo Shumman (1757–1820). *Botan* and *enshika*, peonies
and irises. Inscribed with poems. With a fan-shaped seal: *Karen kusaki awase
Shumman sei*, a collection of plants done for the Mist Club by Shumman.
20.6 × 18.1 cms (8.1 × 7.1″). E.12–1895

▷ PLATE 23   Katsushika Hokusai (1760–1849). *Kawasemi, ayame* and *nadeshiko*,
kingfisher, irises and pinks, from the series often called the 'Small Flowers'
Inscribed with a poem. Publisher's mark, censor's seal. Signed *Zen Hokusai
Iitsu hitsu. c.* 1830. 22.9 × 16.5 cms (9 × 6.5″). E.599–1899

Even if we confine our attention to his prints and ignore his illustrated books, drawings and paintings, the artistic output of Hokusai
during the years 1825–1833 is truly amazing. In addition to the
Thirty-Six Views of Mount Fuji (in fact there are 46 in all), he published sets of ghost stories, famous bridges, waterfalls and Chinese
and Japanese poets as well as two floral series, one with flowers alone
and the other with birds added (PLATE 23). In fact almost all of his
work which is well-known in the West was produced in this short
period of less than a decade. Hokusai was always seeking to broaden
the horizons of his art and although both landscapes and bird-and-
flower prints (*kachōe*) had been designed by earlier *ukiyoe* artists it
was he who elevated both of them to the status of major areas of
subject matter, on a par with courtesans and actors.

The search for new themes during the nineteenth century led to
the rise of the warrior print, whose greatest master was Utagawa
Kuniyoshi (PLATES 24 and 25). He was another fascinatingly many-
sided individual, who studied a huge range of artists and styles (including, like Hokusai, European painting which he discovered
through prints brought to Japan by Dutch traders) and tried his
hand at every conceivable type of subject. But in spite of his landscapes and his Chinese legends, with their European-looking per-
spective and shading, he continues to be admired most of all for his
warrior prints. As his celebrated heroic triptychs lose so much when
reduced in size, we have chosen for reproduction a single sheet print
(PLATE 24) from a series produced during one of his most fertile
periods. Kuniyoshi's skill in depicting violent and sanguinary con-
flict is self-evident. His interest in the past was, however, by no
means confined to warfare and around 1840 he published a fine
series of prints of some of the 'Hundred Poets' (PLATE 25). These
poets were the authors of a hundred poems selected in 1235 by the
famous Fujiwara no Sadaie (often called Teika) and it is clear that
in designing the series Kuniyoshi was conscious of the classical
nature of the subject. Especially in his depiction of figures in court
dress and his choice of colours, his debt to the narrative scrolls of
the mediaeval period is very evident.

Kuniyoshi had many pupils, some of whom produced work of
feeble quality and quite staggering dullness but in Yoshitoshi (PLATE
26) he had a worthy successor. As this posthumously published print
shows, the printers of the Meiji period (1868–1912) reached new
heights of technical expertise: the water which surrounds the two
combatants is suggested by streaks of chemical blue whose delicate
shading must have required very painstaking blockcutting and care-
ful wiping of the ink before printing. The ferocious expressions and
the elaborately detailed blockcarving represent the ultimate development of the style inaugurated by Kuniyoshi.

PLATE 24
Utagawa Kuniyoshi (1797–1861)
The warrior-monk *Negoro no
Komizucha* amid a hail of weapons,
number 26 from the series
Taiheiki Eiyūden, stories of
outstanding bravery in the
16th century wars
Narrative text by *Ryūkatei
Tanekazu* (1807–1858)
Publisher's mark, censors' seals
Signed *Ichiyūsai Kuniyoshi ga*
1847–1850
35.3 × 25 cms (13.9 × 9.8″)
E.10799–1886

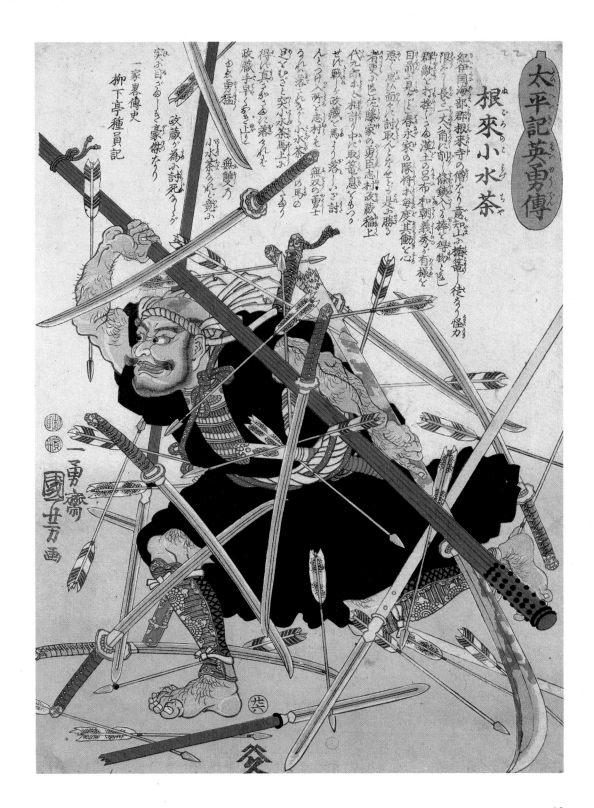

40

PLATE 25
Utagawa Kuniyoshi (1797–1861)
Arihara no Narihira Ason watching
maple leaves floating down the
Tatsuta river, number 17 from the
series *Hyakunin isshu no uchi*, a
hundred poems by a hundred
poets
Publisher's mark
Signed *Chōrō Kuniyoshi ga* with
seal-mark
c. 1840–1842
35.9 × 24.1 cms (14.1 × 9.5″)
E.11411–1886

PLATE 26
Tsukioka Yoshitoshi (1839–1892)
Rōrihakuchō Chōjun and *Kokusempū
Riki* fighting underwater, a scene
from the novel *Suikoden*, a
translation of the Chinese novel
Shui hu chuan, 'The Water
Margin'
Publisher's inscription
Signed *Kaisai Yoshitoshi ga* with a
seal *Taiso*
1900
71.1 × 24.4 cms (28 × 9.6″)
E.1028–1914   Noguchi Gift

PLATE 27 Yamada Kuniteru (1829–1874) *Tōkyō Nihombashi no kei*, a view of
Nihon bridge, Tokyo. Publisher's marks, censor's seals. Signed *Ichiyōsai Kuniteru ga* and
motome ni ōjite, by special request, *Kuniteru ga.* 1870. 36.3 × 70.4 cms (14.3 × 27.7″)
E.99–1969 Shelving Bequest

PLATE 28 ? Tsukioka Kōgyo (1869–1927). A squadron of our destroyers engages in close and bitter fighting with an enemy battleship outside Port Arthur and inflicts a major defeat on April 13th 1904. Publisher's inscription
Signed ? Kōkyo and *motome ni ōjite*, by special request, with an undeciphered seal
Published April 20th 1904. 38.1 × 76.2 cms (15 × 30″). E.3140–1905

In 1854 a treaty was signed between the United States and Japan and two ports were opened to American trade; the other great powers quickly followed suit and soon the wholesale westernisation and modernisation of Japan was in full swing. In 1868 the power of the emperor was restored and the capital was renamed Tokyo. Foreigners appeared on the streets of the great cities and western-style carriages and omnibuses came into use. The opportunities afforded by this novel subject-matter prevented the landscape print from going into total decline, as Kuniteru's interesting scene shows (PLATE 27).

Japanese block-carvers worked fast and actor portraits usually came out within a few days of the first performance of a play. This speed of production was utilised for the last time during the Sino–Japanese (1894–5) and Russo–Japanese (1904–5) wars, when a number of obscure artists, among them Kōkyo or Kōgyo (PLATE 28), were employed to produce stirringly patriotic scenes of military valour and efficiency which were on sale in Tokyo within as little as a week of the action taking place.

Leaping on half a century we come to the work of Munakata Shikō (PLATE 29), the greatest exponent of the modern print movement. All the conventions of the old prints of Edo are cast aside by this pugnacious artist, who was born far from Tokyo in the often-snowbound northernmost part of Honshu, the main island of Japan. After a youthful dalliance with western painting techniques, Munakata decided in the late 1920s that he should return to an essentially Japanese method of self-expression and he rapidly created a new and personal style whose main features are great boldness and, very often, profound religious intensity. His imaginative vitality bodes well for the Japanese print which is at present enjoying a powerful, many-sided and one hopes, long-lived revival.

Books for Further Reading

The literature of the Japanese print is enormous and only a few of the most essential books in English are mentioned here. The largest selection of prints from the Victoria and Albert Museum's own collections will be found in R. A. Crighton, *The Floating World, Japanese popular prints 1700–1900*, London, 1973, where about three hundred are reproduced with useful captions. A good if somewhat old-fashioned general introduction, which combines thorough scholarship with interesting aesthetic judgements, is Laurence Binyon and J. J. O'Brien Sexton, *Japanese Colour Prints*, London, 1923 and 1960. Richard Lane, *Images from the Floating World*, Oxford, 1978, is a more up-to-date survey, but there is an unnecessarily strong emphasis on *shunga* and some of the opinions expressed are eccentric. The book includes a 150 page *Illustrated Dictionary of* Ukiyo-e, which contains much useful information, some of it drawn from other secondary sources. Other good general works (both of them consisting of full-page illustrations with extensive commentaries) are Narazaki Muneshige, *The Japanese Print: its Evolution and Essence*, Tokyo, 1966 and Harold P. Stern, *Master Prints of Japan*, New York, 1969. The text of the latter book is particularly lively and sensitive. For an example of in-depth cataloguing displaying profound knowledge of the literary, social and theatrical background of each print illustrated, David Waterhouse, *Images of Eighteenth-Century Japan*, Toronto, 1975, is recommended. A superb catalogue of a great collection is Jack Hillier, *Japanese Prints and Drawings from the Vever Collection*, London, 1976, which has nearly a thousand entries. For biographical details of artists the best reference book is L. P. Roberts, *A Dictionary of Japanese Artists*, New York and Tokyo, 1976. The coverage of the print artists is excellent: characters are given for all the different names and where there is factual uncertainty the different scholarly opinions are set out. There is also an extensive bibliography.

Works on individual artists are recommended as follows (in alphabetical order of artist):

Jack Hillier, *Suzuki Harunobu*, Philadelphia, 1970.
D. B. Waterhouse, *Harunobu and his Age*, London, 1964.
B. W. Robinson, *Hiroshige*, London, 1964.
Jack Hillier, *Hokusai*, London, 1955 and 1978.
Chieko Hirano, *Kiyonaga*, Cambridge, Mass., 1939.
B. W. Robinson, *Kuniyoshi*, London, 1961.
Jack Hillier, *Utamaro*, London, 1961 and 1979.

The following specialist works are recommended:

David Chibbett, *The History of Japanese Printing and Book Illustration*, Tokyo, New York and San Francisco, 1977.
M. Ishida, *Japanese Buddhist Prints*, Tokyo, 1964.
M. Kawakita, *Contemporary Japanese Prints*, Tokyo, 1967.
R. S. Keyes and Keiko Mizushima, *The Theatrical World of Osaka Prints*, Philadelphia, 1973.
K. Meissner, *Surimono*, London, n.d. (*c.* 1970).
O. Statler, *Modern Japanese Prints*, Rutland, Vermont and Tokyo, 1956.
T. Yoshida and R. Yuki, *Japanese Print-Making*, Rutland, Vermont and Tokyo, 1966. Deals with contemporary and traditional techniques.

Index of Artists

Figures in normal type refer to page numbers, those in italics to plate numbers.